I WISH I MAY

I WISH I MIGHT

Leo Rhodes Jr

Printed in the USA by:
Credits: Book designed by Laeila Gordon and Vonnie Williams

Compiled by Annie L. Ford Yancey
Writerwrite19@gmail.com

Acknowledgements

I would like to acknowledge God who blessed me with talent to write the class of poetry I write. I would like to acknowledge my stepmother, Enetta Rhodes, who planted seeds of wisdom in my life. I acknowledge my grandparents, Thelma and Savana Rhodes, who instilled in me the ability to soul search.

Table of Contents

Man

Isn't it an honor and a privilege to be in this universe?

In this galaxy,

In this solar system,

On this planet,

In this country,

In this state and in this city

As a human being?

Made in God's own image. Perfectly designed without blemish.

A man is good. A man can be crude. A man is cool, but he could be rude.

Men are spectacular. Men are great; only through God can they create.

Men are gentle with certain things thereof, knowing when to be strong and when to give love.

A creative creature man is, whose evidence is seen far and near.

I'm A Poet

My only tools are paper and pen.

I use them over and over again. I'm a Poet.

My thoughts within are where it all begins.

Together with thoughts, paper, and pen turns a poet.

I turn a poet for you to read. If you seem to like it, yes indeed,

you can show it.

I'm just a guy with nothing to do

But think and turn poet in my mind for you.

Cause thinking of you makes me write a poem

In good taste to a sweet delight.

When I write makes my whole day bright.

I'm your poet.

I can write in rhythm any way I want to, like a poet.

Think of me and I'll be thinking of you when I poet.

That's when poetry is easy to write.

Our thoughts together make thinking just right.

To me, it's better than flying a kite. I'm a poet.

Ha Ha He He

Ha Ha He He laughter to me is graceful as can be.

Ha Ha He He, that's what I say to the funniness that I see.

Ha Ha He He a joyful noise, whether from a he or she.

Ha Ha He He may have started around one million years B.C.

A verbal response to what's been heard when someone mentions a joke of words.

When a finger tickles in your side.

A verbal response to what you see with your eyes.

Ha Ha He He look at the clown when from the ring he flee.

Ha Ha He He he's funny to me, my laughter guarantee.

Ha Ha He He, this poem is funny, tell me do you agree?

Ha Ha He He come on try it, it's easy as one, two, three.

So, let's go Ha Ha He He He He Ha Ha Ha Ha He He Ha Ha!

Everyone laughs in their own unique way when everything going Aye ok.

Now and then everyone should laugh, at least that's what the doctors say,

And when I'm really tickled, I laugh this way

Ha Ha He He He He Ha Ha Ha Ha He He Ha Ha!

Mother's Love

There's nothing more precious than a mother's love.

A love that is sanctioned from heaven above.

Nothing can replace the love of a mother.

A maternal connection between a sister or a brother.

Some call her Mom, some call her Mama, some call her Mother, some call her Mudea.

There's nothing more precious than a mother's love.

A mother's love is pure.

A mother's love is sure.

A mother's love will cure and is bound to endure.

A mother's love has got what it takes.

A mother's love will not forsake.

There's nothing more precious than a mother's love.

Thank You

There comes a time when hope rises for the wise.

A time of joy we all surmise.

There comes a time when Mother Earth brings forth her produce for what it's worth.

It's a time to be thankful on this Thanksgiving Day.

Thank you for the harvest that we all need.

Thank you for the rain, yes indeed. With your love and blessings, we're bound to succeed.

Thank you, God, for Jesus. Thank you for my life, my job, my home, and my wife.

Thank you for rescuing me when times were urgent, for washing my mind with your divine detergent.

With you, there's peace of mind for the young and old. The fact that you, Lord, are in control.

Thank you, God for everything.

Nobody Listens When I Speak

Nobody listens when I speak.

Is it because my voice is weak?

Or is it because they don't like what I say,

Which opposes the reality I'm trying to display?

On the negative side, not meaning no harm,

Except when displayed to me; that's when feelings get warm.

But on the positive side, I've learned to keep my cool.

For you don't get to be old being a fool.

Nobody listens when I speak.

Even when holding a conversation.

Maybe it's the politics surrounding the situation.

Like going through one ear and out the other

When I'm talking one to another.

If I'm to whom it may concern,

I, of course, have got to say something.

But it seems I'm just talking loud and saying nothing.

Why don't they listen when I speak?

Do they realize that I'm here?

Or is it what I have to say within their minds they fear?

Nobody listens when I speak.

To me, it just don't sccm right.

Maybe because they don't want to listen, and if that's the case, then the truth is light!

Pump It

You've already heard how to rock it, sock it, and pop it.

So, now let me tell you how to pump it.

Are you ready?

When you're too hot to trot, whether ready or not, you've got to have some. If you feel like stepping and messing around all suited up and tied down, have your night out on the town and party.

Style and smile out on the floor holding hands with the one that you adore, they can tell she's your Cherie Amour, the way she shakes it.

Belly to belly and toes to toes, oh what a position for sweet repose; and after the fun with your heart's delight, it's fanny to fanny for the rest of the night to pump it.

All and all, it's cool, but don't break the rules when you do it.

Now grab your lover while you're hot to trot and just blow 'em away like a twelve-gauge pump shot rock it.

I mean, sock it; if you can do it, get to it.

Now there's plenty more where that comes from, and you can have some.

So, let's go, pump it up!

Slam dunk it on down like drilling for oil deep in the ground to strike it!

And if you're strong and bold when you reach your goal, you can't fight it.

So, come on, now, dig to the left; drill to the right.

Bore it out to your heart's delight.

Peaking out is what it's all about. Do you like it?

It won't be long, time will come to pass, don't pump it too slow, don't pump it too fast, and don't stop it.

Now gone and get it.

I see you like it, so just dig on down and dump it.

Oh no, you can't mess around, slam dunk it!

Oh yes, together in any kind of weather, you can bump it. When you need to lust for that feeling, you will get when you pump it.

I Wish I May I Might

I wish

I may

I might

Make a dream come true.

I wish

I may

I might

Sing a song of love to you.

I wish

I may

I might

Wake up with you cuddled next to me, as warm and con-
tented as one could be.

You and I so happy; happy to the third degree.

I wish

I may

I might

Be a waterbed for you.

I wish

I may

I might

Be your cover and your pillow too.

I wish

Someway

I might

Comfort you through and through.

I think I know what's right for you.

A love that's tailored to fit your needs.

A love of your own to do as you please.

As to the subject for which it stands

If I can, and I think I can, become a tool of love for your

satisfaction

To bring out your utmost positive reaction.

I wish

I may

I might

Be your sweet, sweet inspiration.

I wish

Someway

I might

Increase your motivation.

I wish

Someday

I might

Make a hobby of loving you.

There's even more that I might do.

Like fill you up with love and affection

Just to keep you strong and heading in my direction.

My care for you is easy to conceive.

That is a friend in need is a friend indeed.

I wish

I may

I might

Have you here with me tonight

I wish

I may

I might

Let you make me feel alright.

I wish

I may

I might

Wish upon a star of light:

The brightest star I see tonight

I wish I may I wish I might

Have the may I wish tonight!

I wish

I may

I might

Practice Makes Perfect

Practice is the key to winners' traits and the goal they project to achieve.

The thrill of victory would indicate; they're the best in their minds; they believe.

To perform when it's time to show. True lovers are good to go.

Although it may seem like a fantasy, you're feeling so good, realistically.

Reaching the peak so climatically because practice makes perfect lovingly.

Practice makes perfect! Now that's the player's way to be always prepared for display

Their special techniques are in tune and on time through practice, the old-fashioned way!

Every move that's made intentionally is done so precisely and professionally.

May the force be with you continuously, because practice makes perfect, definitely.

To pace the way relentlessly, so cool, calm, and collectively.

Being all the things that you can be, the epitome of our society.

Stand up to be recognized, so everyone can see that practice makes perfect, obviously.

Practice makes perfect at loving you, Boo. Understand all that I say?

That's right, it ripens like wine over a period of time, from loving you day after day.

Sometimes I might do desperately, the things I do affectionately.

I'm an all the way lover inparticularly, and practice makes perfect, indubitably.

Story Of Love

Some people say that love can be blue.

Now that can be false, or it could be true.

Depending on who God has in store for you.

Some people's philosophy behind love, you see, is one plus one equals three.

Some say it also equals two, depending on who you're giving it to.

Love, like life, has its breaks.

To couple up means you got what it takes.

To couple up to be together alone and treat each other like a precious stone.

A very nice situation for such a great sensation, yielding to each other's love demonstrations.

By now, one to another might say, "For us, it's such a lovely day."

"The sun so bright and the sky so blue." "How sweet it is to be loved by you." "How sweet it is to have a love so true".

Behold, you're in love again, to one who's a companion as well as a friend.

Now, your heart is in the sky.

Love has made you feel so high.

Just floating along on a breeze, feeling so good, at peace, at ease.

Love, I guess, can be very sweet.

Love can also make you weep.

Then there's a change in the wind.

Love has suddenly come to an end.

A love that started to be a ball is suddenly headed for a great big fall.

Down! Down! All the way down to that sudden stop when love hits the ground.

Love is scattered all around.

Pieces are found in the north, south, east, and the west.

It's a pity how a four-letter word can make such a mess.

Love is shattered.

Left sitting heartbroken within, as many teardrops fall off your chin,

You try to put love together again.

Like in Humpty Dumpty and all the King's men.

So many pieces, so small, so few.

So much work in store for you.

It makes you feel like it's really a drag.

It makes you feel as if you've been had.

But you know for love just what it takes, with grace from God, for goodness' sake.

You pick up the pieces and mend love's breaks.

Pick up the pieces and mend love breaks.

Mend loves breaks.

Easier Said Than Done

Whether up or down, don't be messing around.

Whether high or low, it's not what you know but who you know.

My name is Leo, not Nintendo nor piano.

I'm the third degree, bold as can be.

I'm so bad I scare me.

The star of the show being as young as I am, you know.

Don't make me thirty-eight hot.

If you tick me off, I'll blow my nose and slap you with my snot.

Do that thing or get up off the pot and put a break check on doing your thing.

You never know what the next five minutes might bring, and stop that tweaking;

Tweaking out on life.

Check Speed!

Check Fuel!

Check your six!

Break check!

And check yourself before you wreck yourself, all or none.

Anything worth having is hard to get and is easier said than done.

If it ain't one thang, it's three thangs.

If it ain't this thang, it's that thang.

If it ain't the other thang, it's another thang.

Seems like it's always something.

Old bad habits are hard to break by n by.

A thousand times I ask myself why is it so hard to come together right now over me, myself & I.

Nothing beats a failure but a try.

Don't let life pass you by.

Even if you got to crawl before you walk: walk before you run;

It's easier said than done.

Play

Play little boy with your favorite toy.

Careful not to break it: it's the one you enjoy.

Play little girl with your little rag doll.

Take care of her with those pretty blue eyes.

A doll of love upon which you strive.

A doll to love you, you believe is alive.

Play house with a friend while the parents' away.

Playing with a friend somehow led both astray.

Just so house, the two may play.

As young as they are, they say it's ok.

So now both are being bad.

For instance, she is the Mama and he is the Dad.

A child is born dumb; they truly don't know. For everything a child learns, someone had to show.

So play house, little kids, until your heart's content.

Play and be happy one hundred percent. Whether wrong or right, you do not know if your parents can't say they told you so.

One time, you saw what grownups do: you figure what's right for them is right for you too.

Play with it.

The Antichrist

As it is written since the beginning, for what it's worth, to wonder why the best laid plans of mice and man oftentimes go asunder.

It is forbidden, as it is written, to have other Gods before Him.

The Lord thy God is a jealous God and no other God before.

The Antichrist.

The Antichrist: He is to blame for plagues, wars, rumors of wars, and life just not the same.

The opposite of wrong is right.

For our souls, we have to fight; sensation, tribulation, frustration, and temptation.

Sometimes it's hard to do what's right.

What a bird does best is fly.

What a fish does best is swim.

What a winner does best is win,

and what a sinner does best is sin.

All are doing what comes naturally in accordance with the way they were made.

But it was God who created the birds and the fish, and the price for our sins he paid. That's right!

The Antichrist.

The Antichrist: it's a crying shame.

Rebuke him in Jesus' name and send him back to hell from whence he came.

The world was left devastated from Omicron to COVID.

Millions dead throughout the land left the world in dismay.

Now, I don't know about you, but I will never ever forget all the lost souls around the globe. I don't know what to say except, the Antichrist: the Antichrist cursed is his name.

Why? To conquer the souls of all mankind through evil is in vain.

Introduction to Son of God

Through trials, tribulations, and the aftermath thereof, plus indignations from the chambers of mystery. Opposes reality, as well as the justice provisions within the minds of mankind.

Son of God

Now this is a poem that I'd like to toast to Jesus Christ, whom I love the most.

Only he stood out from all the rest, as proof he passed the ultimate test.

The Son of God in man's state of reality. I'd say blessed is this man from Galilee.

His mission, to save this world from sin. Mission started the day his life here begin.

Born of the Virgin Mary, who during those times was quite contrary.

A queen of the stock, chosen at God's discretion, from the flock of women within his worldly possession.

A heavenly man with a heart so dear; so much was his uniqueness, in some minds, made fear. "Believe not what ye yet understand," express some priests to others.

"No better is this man as is to another."

What he had to say, they'd rather people not know.

What he had to display, they didn't want him to show.

They heard he healed those who are sickly and blue, and He believed in things they didn't want others to.

Why they felt, "Jesus Christ a superstar: "Hah!" Now just who in this world do you think you are?"

Just to show all who they thought was the boss, they beat our savior and nailed him to a cross.

So, crucified on earth was the Son of God.

While followers on their knees prayed to the Lord.

They feared to suffer what thought was the end. They prayed to his death, for he was a friend.

His body carried to a tomb and stored within. To reassure all who believe in him, Christ rises again.

For God so loved the world, he gave his only begotten Son; that whosoever believeth in him shall not perish but have everlasting life.

Praise the Lord. Hallelujah!

Favor Isn't Fair

By Derricka Lee

Tragic awoke me inside a bed not mine.

Behind my closed eyes, I felt a shadow. Awakened to see myself inside a hospital room.

Seeing my mother there in tears, with my pastor by her side, but wait, not to mention, a girl who I thought was my friend, but really Satan in disguise.

Surrounded by all three, I suddenly remembered what just happened to me.

Knowing the answers in the back of my mind.

Not because I'm black, or because I have beautiful eyes, but because I am a child of God is why I've reached this point in my life.

Face swollen; an eye that's black; with a jaw that's broken and cracked, missing a tooth, with a mind that's so confused, trying so hard to understand life situations; asking from the very bottom of my soul, why me?

I know things happen for reasons, but this is difficult for me to accept.

Not knowing whether it was good or bad, a punishment or reward, to get my attention, or to destroy.

Days went by, and I'm still in that bed.

So many thoughts running in and out of my head.

Trying to understand how a person can harm a person with a heart like mine;

Love is all I knew how to show, and to forgive, to forgive is all I know.

Seeing another soul cry was a vision that made me very weak, so immediately, my heart says "help," and that's where I forget all about myself.

A good heart, got me lying still so

What do I do? Where do I go? That is what my flesh screams out!!!

But my soul, my soul cries out,

Yes, Lord, I hear your voice,

As the tears fall from my face and my heart beating with agony and pain, all I could do now is call on your name. You know my heart, please renew my mind.

I know you have all the answers to all the questions I'm seeking;

So, I harden not my heart, and strap on the armor of God, for this is your battle, Dear Lord; Before I depart, I would like to say thank you. Lord, I thank you for countless things. Thank you for protecting me,

Thank you for the storm, now I know I have a blessing arriving.

Thank you for a praying mother;

She never left my bedside. Thank you for just being you.

Before I depart, I would like to say:

I have learned not yet all, but some of the lessons you have set before me, and all I ask is that you forgive me for all my inequalities and take my hands into yours, for it's you I will serve.

Your very own,

Derricka Lee

Psalms 27